Every day's a Handwriting day with CGP!

Learning how to write neatly is a really important skill in Year 1, and the only way to tackle it is practice, practice and more practice...

That's where this CGP book comes in. It's packed with bright and colourful handwriting exercises for every day of autumn term.

And of course, we've included helpful guidelines and plenty of examples — perfect for sharpening up pupils' handwriting skills, one day at a time!

What CGP is all about

Our sole aim here at CGP is to produce the highest quality books — carefully written, immaculately presented and dangerously close to being funny.

Then we work our socks off to get them out to you — at the cheapest possible prices.

Contents

☑ Use the tick boxes to help keep a record of which pages have been attempted.

Week 1
- ☑ Day 1 1
- ☑ Day 2 2
- ☑ Day 3 3
- ☑ Day 4 4
- ☑ Day 5 5

Week 2
- ☑ Day 1 6
- ☑ Day 2 7
- ☑ Day 3 8
- ☑ Day 4 9
- ☑ Day 5 10

Week 3
- ☑ Day 1 11
- ☑ Day 2 12
- ☑ Day 3 13
- ☑ Day 4 14
- ☑ Day 5 15

Week 4
- ☑ Day 1 16
- ☑ Day 2 17
- ☑ Day 3 18
- ☑ Day 4 19
- ☑ Day 5 20

Week 5
- ☑ Day 1 21
- ☑ Day 2 22
- ☑ Day 3 23
- ☑ Day 4 24
- ☑ Day 5 25

Week 6
- ☑ Day 1 26
- ☑ Day 2 27
- ☑ Day 3 28
- ☑ Day 4 29
- ☑ Day 5 30

Week 7
- ☑ Day 1 31
- ☑ Day 2 32
- ☑ Day 3 33
- ☑ Day 4 34
- ☑ Day 5 35

Week 8
- ☑ Day 1 36
- ☑ Day 2 37
- ☑ Day 3 38
- ☑ Day 4 39
- ☑ Day 5 40

Week 9

- ☑ Day 1 41
- ☑ Day 2 42
- ☑ Day 3 43
- ☑ Day 4 44
- ☑ Day 5 45

Week 10

- ☑ Day 1 46
- ☑ Day 2 47
- ☑ Day 3 48
- ☑ Day 4 49
- ☑ Day 5 50

Week 11

- ☑ Day 1 51
- ☑ Day 2 52
- ☑ Day 3 53
- ☑ Day 4 54
- ☑ Day 5 55

Week 12

- ☑ Day 1 56
- ☑ Day 2 57
- ☑ Day 3 58
- ☑ Day 4 59
- ☑ Day 5 60

Published by CGP

ISBN: 978 1 78908 542 6

Editors: Eleanor Crabtree, Mary Falkner, Rob Hayman, Sharon Keeley-Holden and Hayley Thompson.
Reviewers: Stephanie Lake and Adele Lemin.

With thanks to Gareth Mitchell and Camilla Sheridan for the proofreading.
With thanks to Jan Greenway for the copyright research.

Cover image and graphics used throughout the book © www.edu-clips.com.

Printed by Elanders Ltd, Newcastle upon Tyne.
Based on the classic CGP style created by Richard Parsons.

Text, design, layout and original illustrations © Coordination Group Publications Ltd. (CGP) 2020
All rights reserved.

Photocopying this book is not permitted, even if you have a CLA licence.
Extra copies are available from CGP with next day delivery • 0800 1712 712 • www.cgpbooks.co.uk

How to Use this Book

- This book contains 60 pages of daily handwriting practice.
- It's split into 12 sections — that's roughly one section for each week of the Year 1 Autumn term.
- A week is made up of 5 pages, so there's one for every school day of the term (Monday – Friday).
- Each page should take about 10 minutes to complete.
- The term starts off with pattern tracing and leads on to letter formation. Once enough letters have been taught, pupils start to consolidate their skills by tracing and copying whole words. Capital letters and numbers are covered later in the book.
- A typical page looks like this:

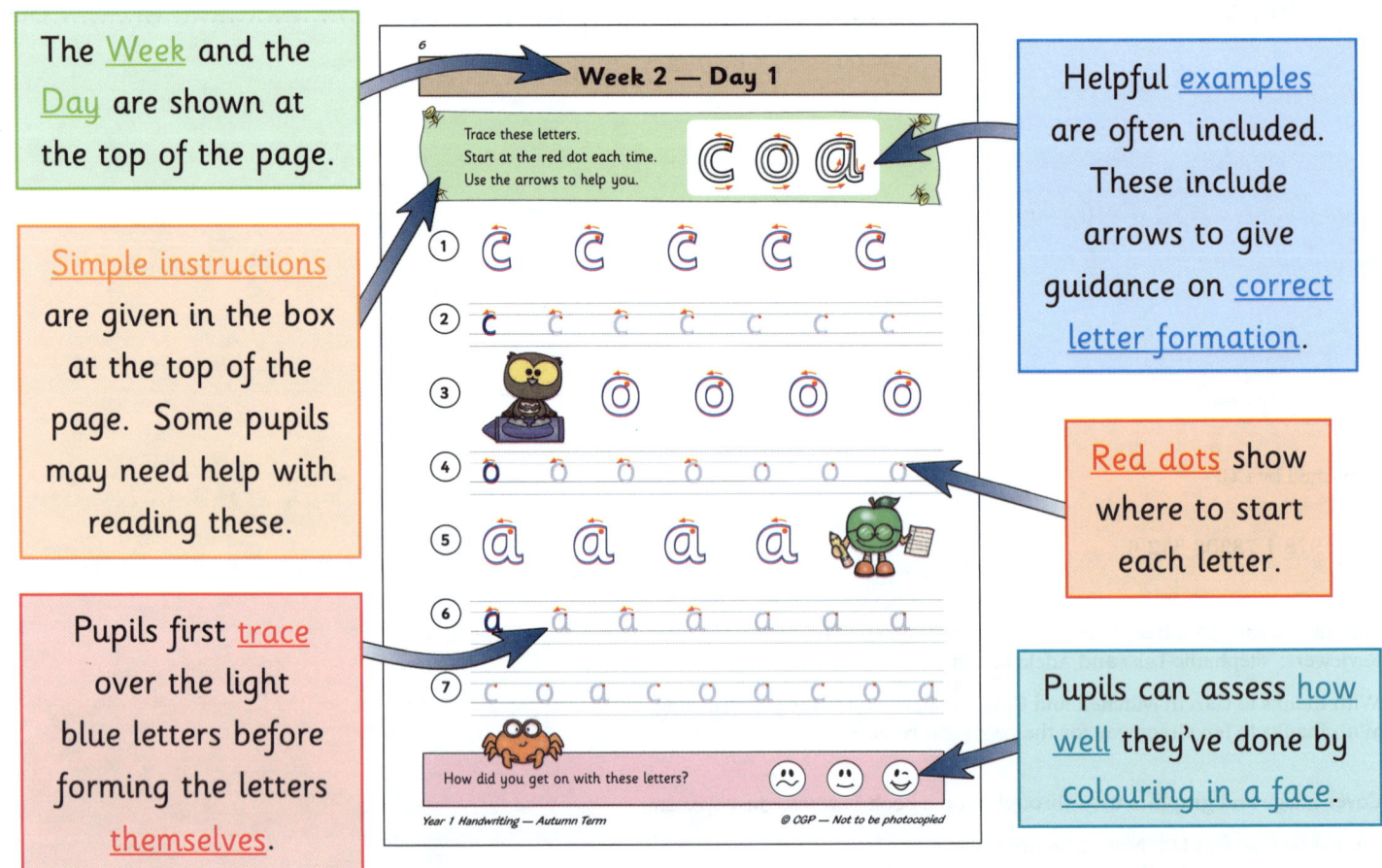

The Week and the Day are shown at the top of the page.

Simple instructions are given in the box at the top of the page. Some pupils may need help with reading these.

Pupils first trace over the light blue letters before forming the letters themselves.

Helpful examples are often included. These include arrows to give guidance on correct letter formation.

Red dots show where to start each letter.

Pupils can assess how well they've done by colouring in a face.

If you are a parent or guardian using this book at home with your child, you should bear in mind that different schools have different handwriting styles (e.g. 'k' instead of 'k'). You should check with the school to see how each letter is written. In this book, some of the letters have flicks at the bottom in preparation for joined-up writing.

Week 1 — Day 1

These patterns are made up of straight lines.
Trace over the pale blue lines with a pencil.

1)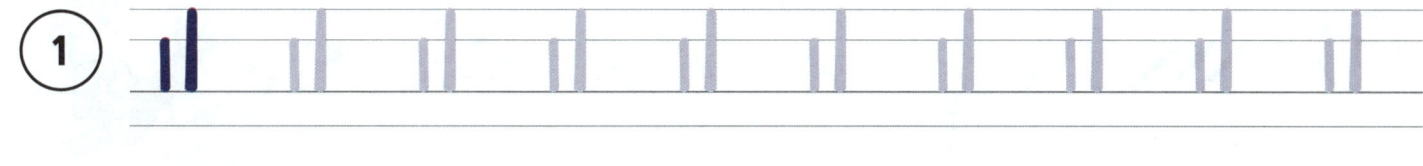

2)

3)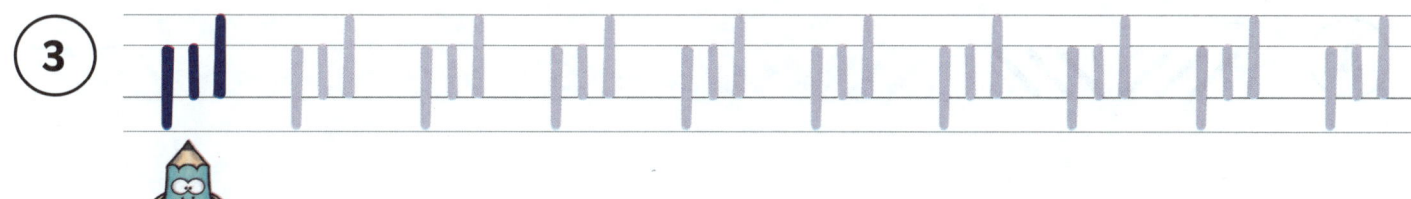

4)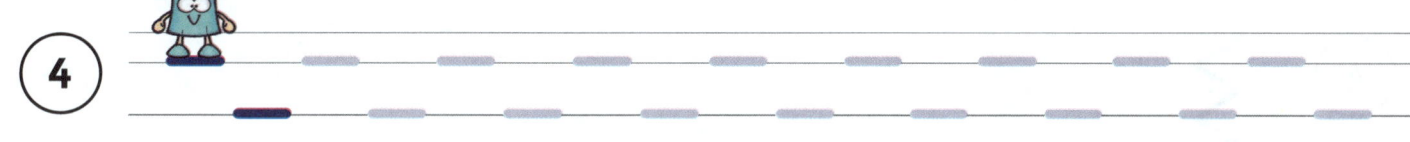

5)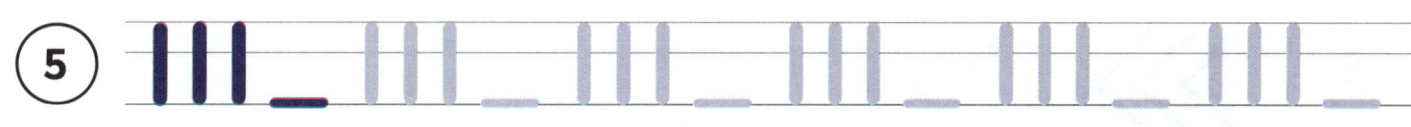

6)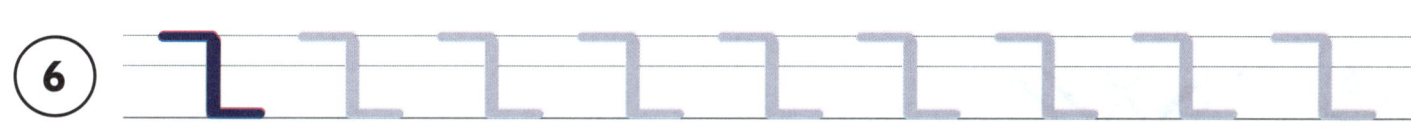

7)

How did you get on with these patterns?

Week 1 — Day 2

These patterns are made up of lines.
Trace over the lines slowly with a pencil.

①

②

③

④

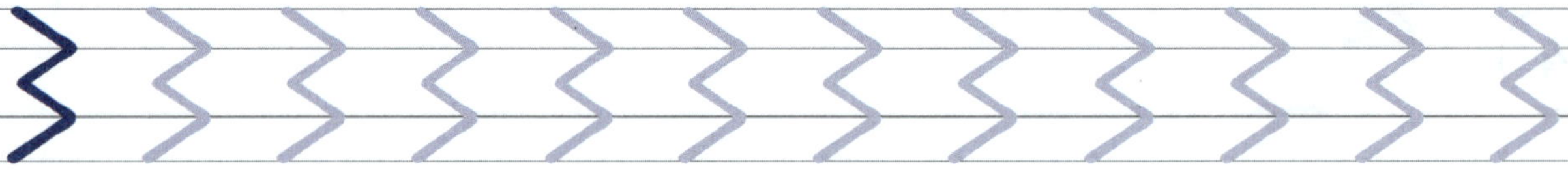

⑤

⑥

⑦

How did you get on with these patterns?

Year 1 Handwriting — Autumn Term

Week 1 — Day 3

These patterns have curved lines.
Trace over them.
Stay as close to the lines as you can.

①

②

③

④

⑤

⑥

⑦

How did you get on with these patterns?

Week 1 — Day 4

Here are some more patterns.
Trace over them with a pencil.

1.

2.

3.

4.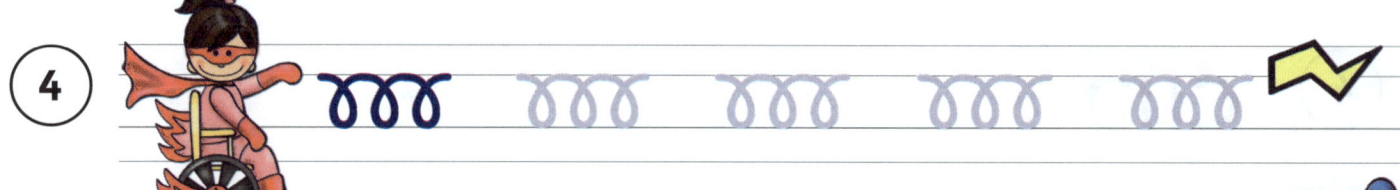

5.

6.

7.

How did you get on with these patterns?

Week 1 — Day 5

Complete this picture by tracing over the light blue lines.

How did you get on with this picture?

Week 2 — Day 1

Trace these letters.
Start at the red dot each time.
Use the arrows to help you.

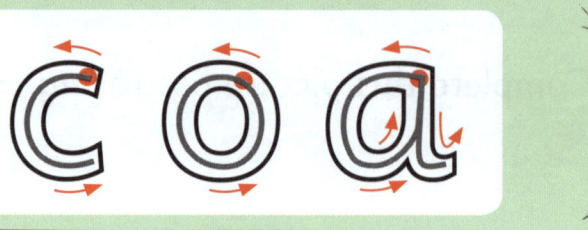

1

2

3

4

5

6

7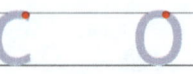

How did you get on with these letters?

Year 1 Handwriting — Autumn Term   © CGP — Not to be photocopied

Week 2 — Day 2

Trace the letters. Then copy them.
Start each letter at the red dot.

c o a

1. c c c c 
2. o o o o
3. a a a a
4. c c c
5. o o o o
6. a a a a
7. a c o

How well did you do with these letters today?

Week 2 — Day 3

Trace the letters. Then copy them. Start each letter at the red dot.

c o a

1. c c
2. o o
3. a a
4. c c
5. o o
6. a a
7. a c o

How did you get on with this page?

Week 2 — Day 4

Trace these letters.
Start at the red dot each time.
Use the arrows to help you.

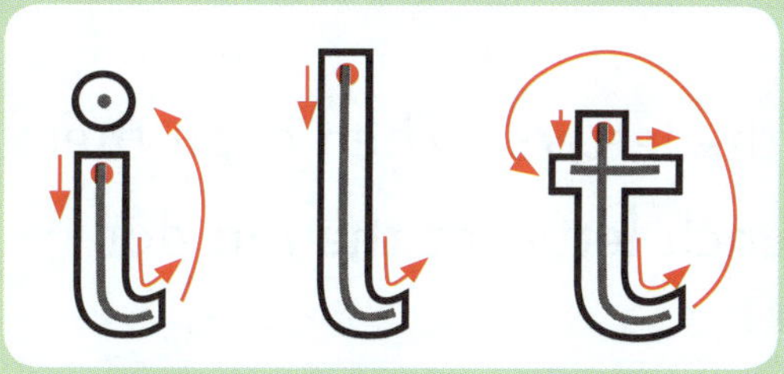

1. i i i i i

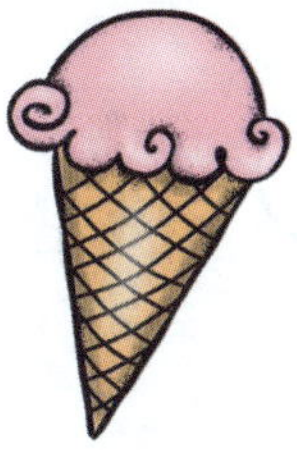

2. i i i i i i i

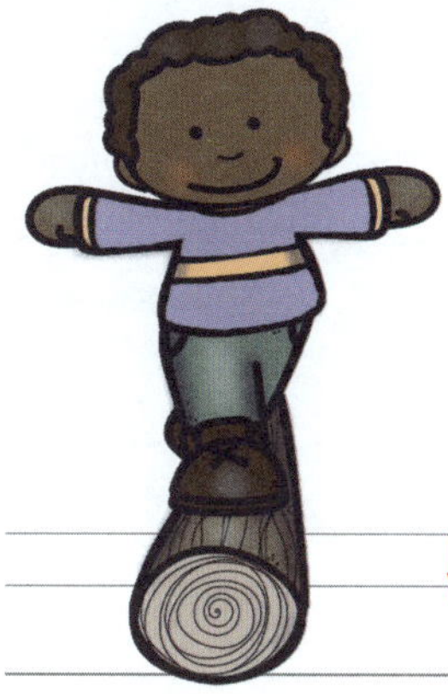

3. l l l l l

4. l l l l l l l

5. t t t t t

6. t t t t t t

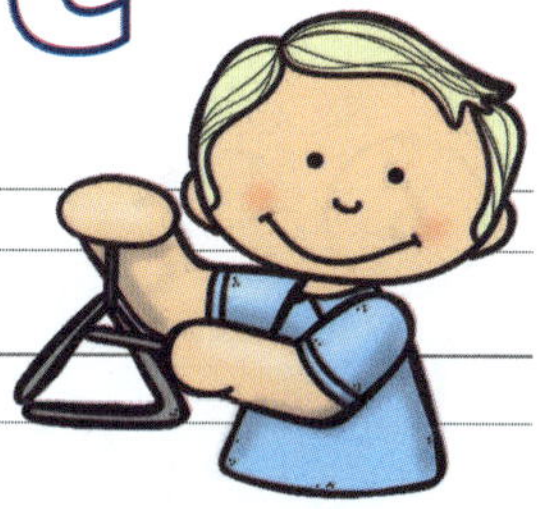

7. i l t i l t i l t

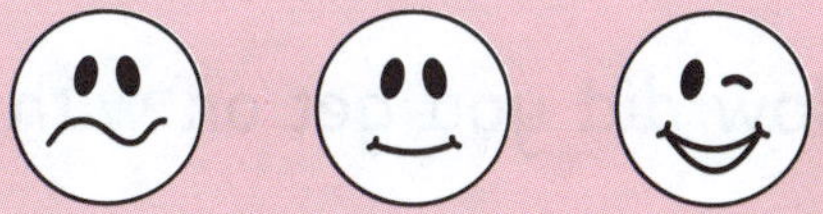

How did you get on with the letters 'i', 'l' and 't'?

Week 3 — Day 1

Trace the letters. Then copy them. Start each letter at the red dot.

1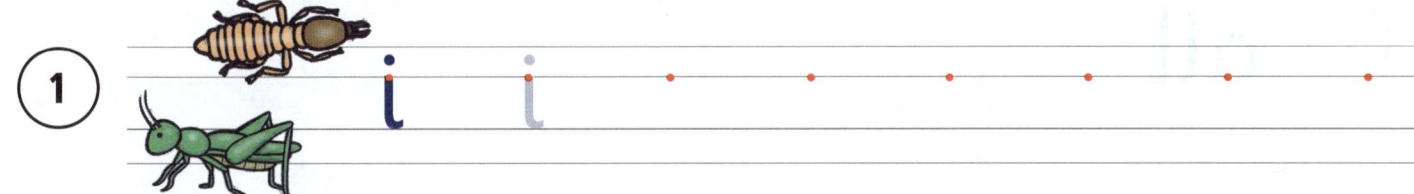

2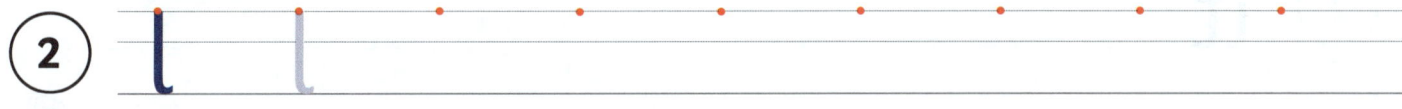

3

4 i i

5

6

7 i l t

How did you get on with these letters?

Week 3 — Day 2

Trace each word. Then copy it.
Start each letter at the red dot.

1. all   all
2. it   it
3. cat   cat
4. lot   lot
5. oil   oil
6. tail   tail
7. coal   coal

How did you get on with these words?

Week 3 — Day 3

Trace each word. Then copy it.
Start each letter at the red dot.

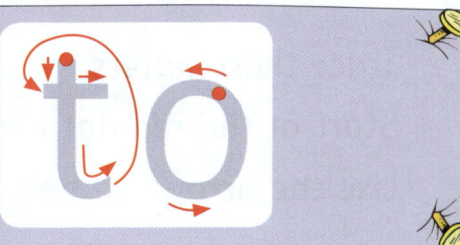

1) to   to

2) at   at

3) cot   cot

4) ill   ill

5) cool   cool

6) coat   coat

7) tool   tool

How did you get on with this page?

Week 3 — Day 4

Trace these letters.
Start at the red dot each time.
Use the arrows to help you.

u y j

1 u u u u

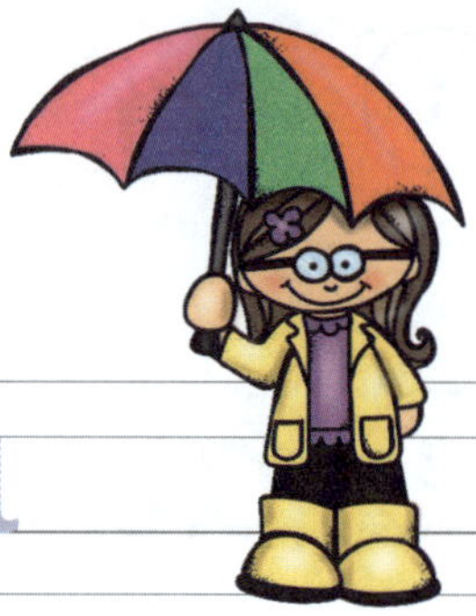

2 u u u u u u

3 y y

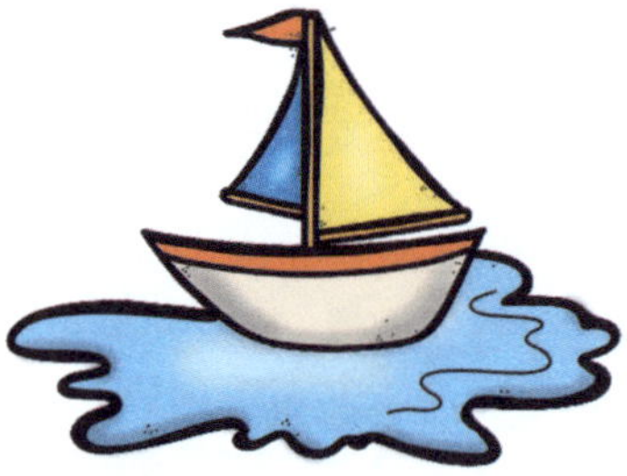

y y

4 y y y y y y y

5 j j j j

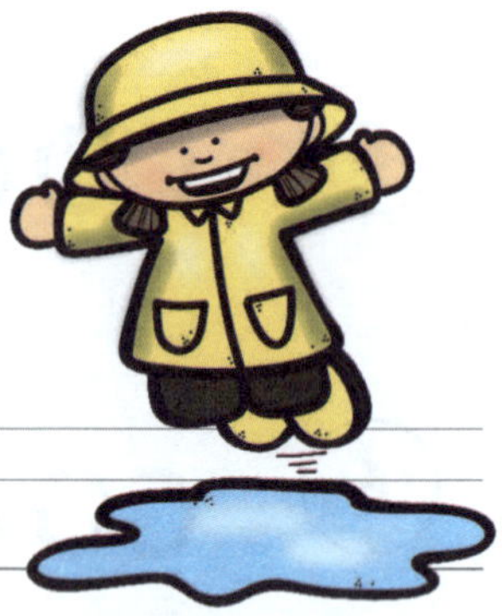

6 j j j j j j

7 u y j u y j u y j

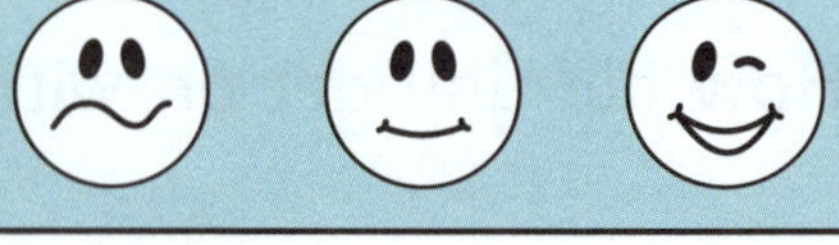

How did you get on with these letters?

Week 3 — Day 5

Trace the letters. Then copy them.
Start each letter at the red dot.

u y j

1. u u u u
2. y y y y
3. j j j j
4. u u u
5. y y y y
6. j j j j
7. u y j

How did you get on with 'u', 'y' and 'j' today?

Week 4 — Day 2

Trace each word. Then copy it.
Start each letter at the red dot.

1) out   out

2) lay   lay

3) joy   joy

4) you   you

5) tutu   tutu

6) clay   clay

7) juicy   juicy

How did you get on with these words?

Week 4 — Day 3

Trace each word. Then copy it out as neatly as you can. Start each letter at the red dot.

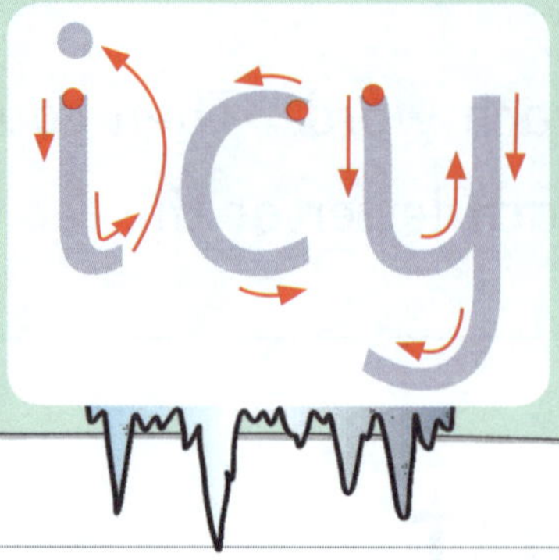

1.  icy   icy
2. cut   cut
3. jot   jot
4. toy   toy 
5. jail   jail
6. city   city
7. jolly jolly

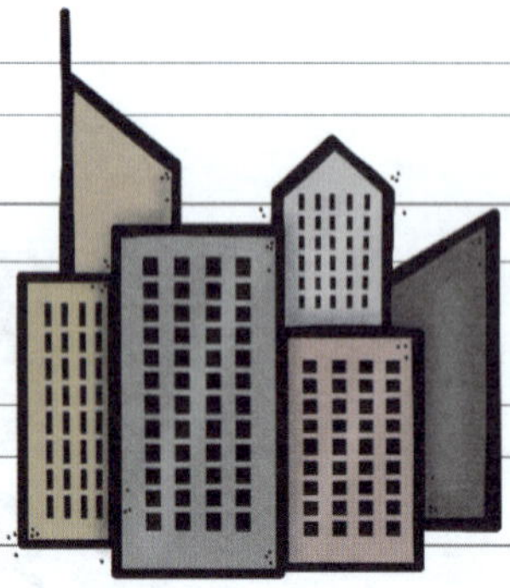

How did you get on with this page?

Year 1 Handwriting — Autumn Term

Week 4 — Day 4

How well did you trace these letters?

Week 4 — Day 5

Trace and copy the letters 'r', 'n', 'm' and 'p'. Start at the red dot each time.

r n m p

1. r r r r
2. n n n n
3. m m m
4. p p p
5. r r n n
6. m m p p
7. r n m p

How did you get on with these letters?

Year 1 Handwriting — Autumn Term

Week 5 — Day 1

Trace each of these letters once.
Then copy them out.

1 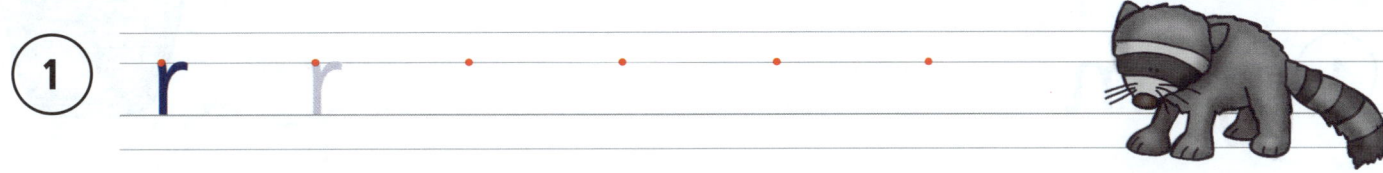 r r

2 n n

3 m m

4 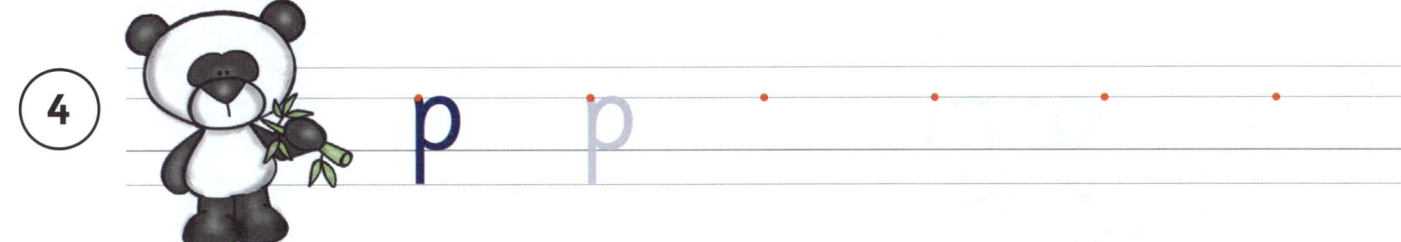 p p

5 r n

6  m p

7 r n m p

Are your letters looking nice and neat?

© CGP — Not to be photocopied Year 1 Handwriting — Autumn Term

Week 5 — Day 2

Trace each word. Then copy it.
Start each letter at the red dot.

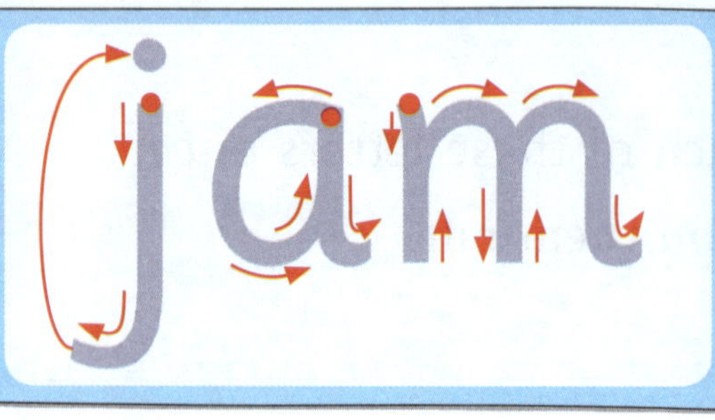

jam

1. jam   jam
2. air   air
3. mint   mint 
4. arm   arm
5. pot   pot
6. port   port
7. corn   corn

How did you find writing these words?

Week 5 — Day 3

Here are seven words to help you practise 'r', 'n', 'm' and 'p'.

1) man   man
2) room   room
3) tuna   tuna
4) rat   rat
5) nap   nap
6) pony   pony
7) lamp   lamp

How did you find writing these words?

Week 5 — Day 4

Trace these letters.
Start at the red dot each time.
Use the arrows to help you.

1. h h h h 
2. h h h h h h h h
3. b b b b 
4. b b b b b b b b
5. k k k k
6. k k k k k k k k
7. h b k h b k h b k

How did you get on with these letters?

Week 5 — Day 5

Start these letters at the top line.
Make sure they finish on the thick line.

h b k

1) h h h h

2) b b b b

3) k k k k

4) h h h h

5) b b b b

6) k k k k

7) h b k

How well do you think you did today?

Week 6 — Day 1

Trace and copy each letter. Use the arrows shown here to help you.

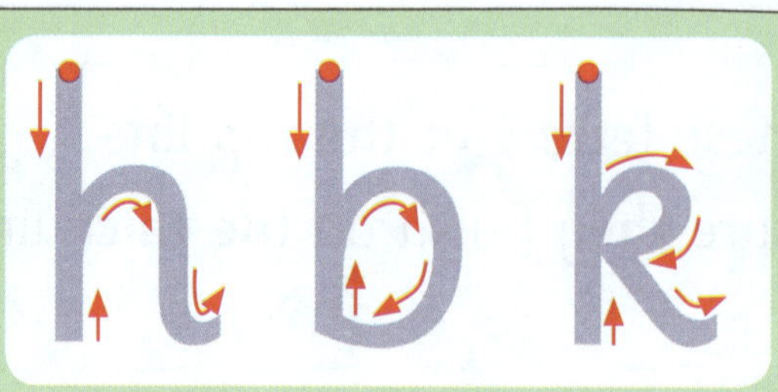

h b k

1.  h h
2. b b 
3. k k
4. h h
5. b b
6. k k 
7. h   b   k

Did you write the letters 'h', 'b' and 'k' neatly?

Week 6 — Day 2

Trace each word on this page.
Then copy it.
Start each letter at a red dot.

1. oak   oak
2. bay   bay
3. lick lick
4. path path
5. bank bank
6. kit   kit
7. harp harp

How well did you do with these words?

Week 6 — Day 3

Trace these words once.
Then write them for yourself.

1. hour   hour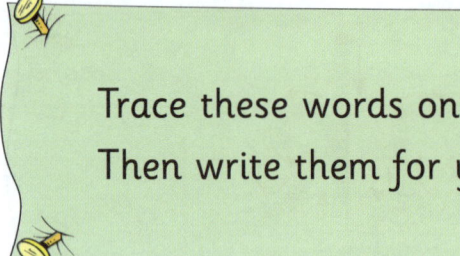

2. back   back

3. hook   hook

4. bath   bath

5. kilt   kilt

6. bump   bump

7. book   book

How neatly did you write these words?

Week 6 — Day 4

Trace these letters. The letters 'g' and 'q' both start off the same. You just change the tail.

1. d d d d
2. d d d d d d d d 
3. g g g g g
4. g g g g g g g
5. q q q q
6. q q q q q q q q 
7. d g q d g q d g q

How did you do with these letters?

Week 6 — Day 5

Trace each of these letters.
Then copy them out yourself.

d g q

1. d d d
2. g g g
3. q q q 
4. d d d 
5. g g g
6. q q q
7. d g q 

How did you get on with these letters?

Week 7 — Day 2

Start each of the letters in these words at the red dots.

1. ring   ring
2. quick   quick
3. goal   goal
4. gang   gang
5. quit   quit
6. mud   mud
7. dark   dark

How well did you do with today's words?

Week 7 — Day 3

Trace these words. Then copy them out. They all contain the letters 'd', 'g' or 'q'.

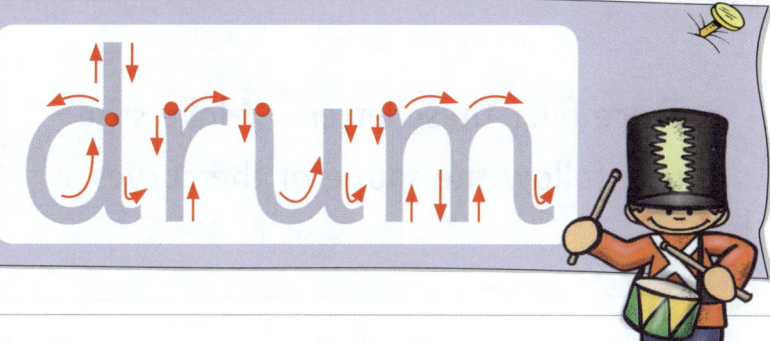

1. drum   drum
2. girl   girl
3. body   body
4. quack   quack
5. drag   drag
6. plug   plug
7. cold   cold

How did today's words go?

Week 7 — Day 4

Trace over these letters. Make sure you follow the shape of the curves.

1. e e e e 
2. e e e e e e
3. s s s s
4. s s s s s s s
5. f f f f f
6. f f f f f f f
7. e s f e s f e s f

How well did you trace the shape of these letters?

Year 1 Handwriting — Autumn Term

Week 7 — Day 5

Trace each of these letters.
Then copy them out yourself.

1. e e e e
2. s s s s 
3. f f f f
4. e e e e
5. s s s s  
6. f f f f
7. e   s   f

How did you find writing these letters?

Week 8 — Day 2

Have a go at tracing and copying these words.

1. end   end
2. fast   fast
3. safe   safe
4. salt   salt
5. fort   fort
6. left   left
7. felt   felt

How did you find writing these words?

Week 8 — Day 3

Trace each of these words. Then copy them. Start each letter at the red dot.

1. eat   eat
2. sand   sand
3. meat   meat
4. feast   feast
5. fresh   fresh
6. test   test
7. food   food

How did you get on with these words?

Week 8 — Day 4

Trace these letters.
Follow the arrows
to help you.

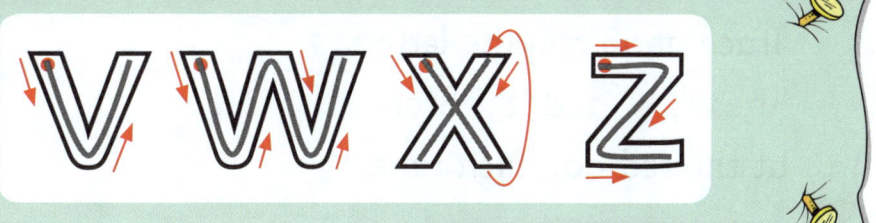

V W X Z

1 V V V W W W

2 v v v v v v

3 w w w w w w

4 X X X Z Z Z

5 x x x x x x x x

6 z z z z z z z z

7 v w x z v w x z

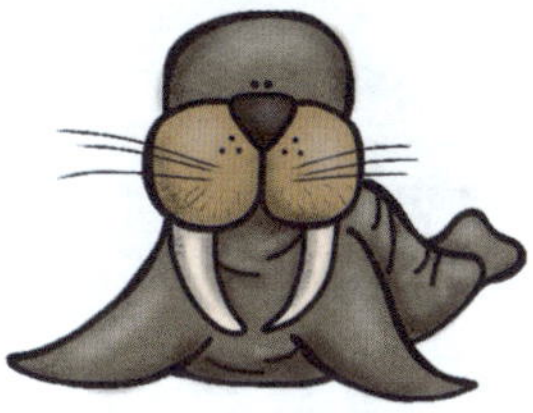

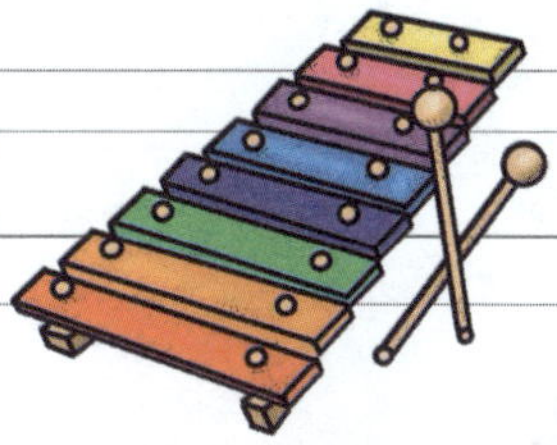

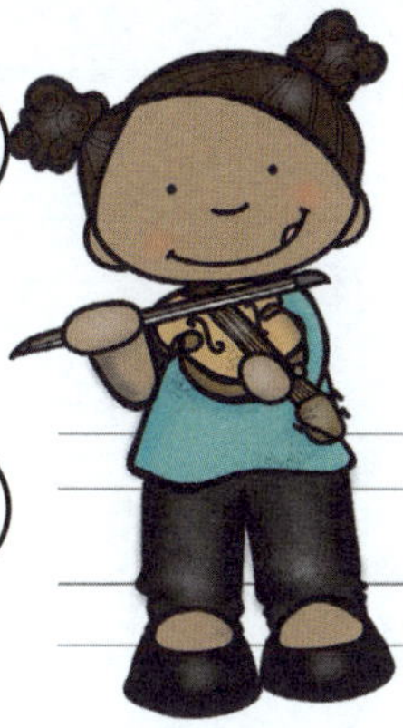

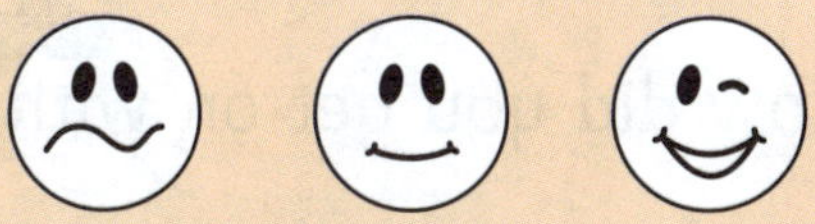

How did you find these letters?

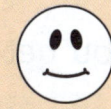

Week 9 — Day 1

Trace each letter. Then copy it out. Start at the red dot each time.

V W X Z

1. V v

2. W w

3. X x

4. Z z

5. v   w

6. x   z

7. v   w   x   z

How did you find copying these letters?

Week 9 — Day 2

Trace each word on the page once. Then copy it out.

1. van van
2. wood wood
3. axe axe
4. taxi taxi
5. zip zip
6. jaw jaw
7. cave cave

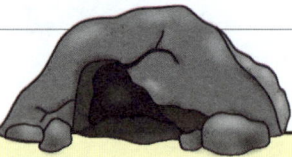

Did you find copying these words easy?

Week 9 — Day 3

Here are seven words containing 'v', 'w', 'x' or 'z'. Trace each word once. Then copy it.

1. wax   wax
2. five   five
3. lava   lava
4. bow   bow
5. jazz   jazz
6. wave   wave
7. lazy   lazy

How did you do with today's words?

Week 9 — Day 4

Trace and copy these capital letters. You will need to lift your pencil off the page for most of them.

1.  A A A A
2. B B B B
3. C C C
4. D D D D
5. E E E E
6. F F F F
7. G G G G

How did you get on with these capital letters?

Year 1 Handwriting — Autumn Term

Week 9 — Day 5

Trace and copy these capital letters. You will need to lift your pencil off the page for most of them.

H I J

1. H H H
2. I I I I 
3. J J J J
4. K K K K
5. L L L L
6. M M M M 
7. N N N N

How did you do with today's capital letters?

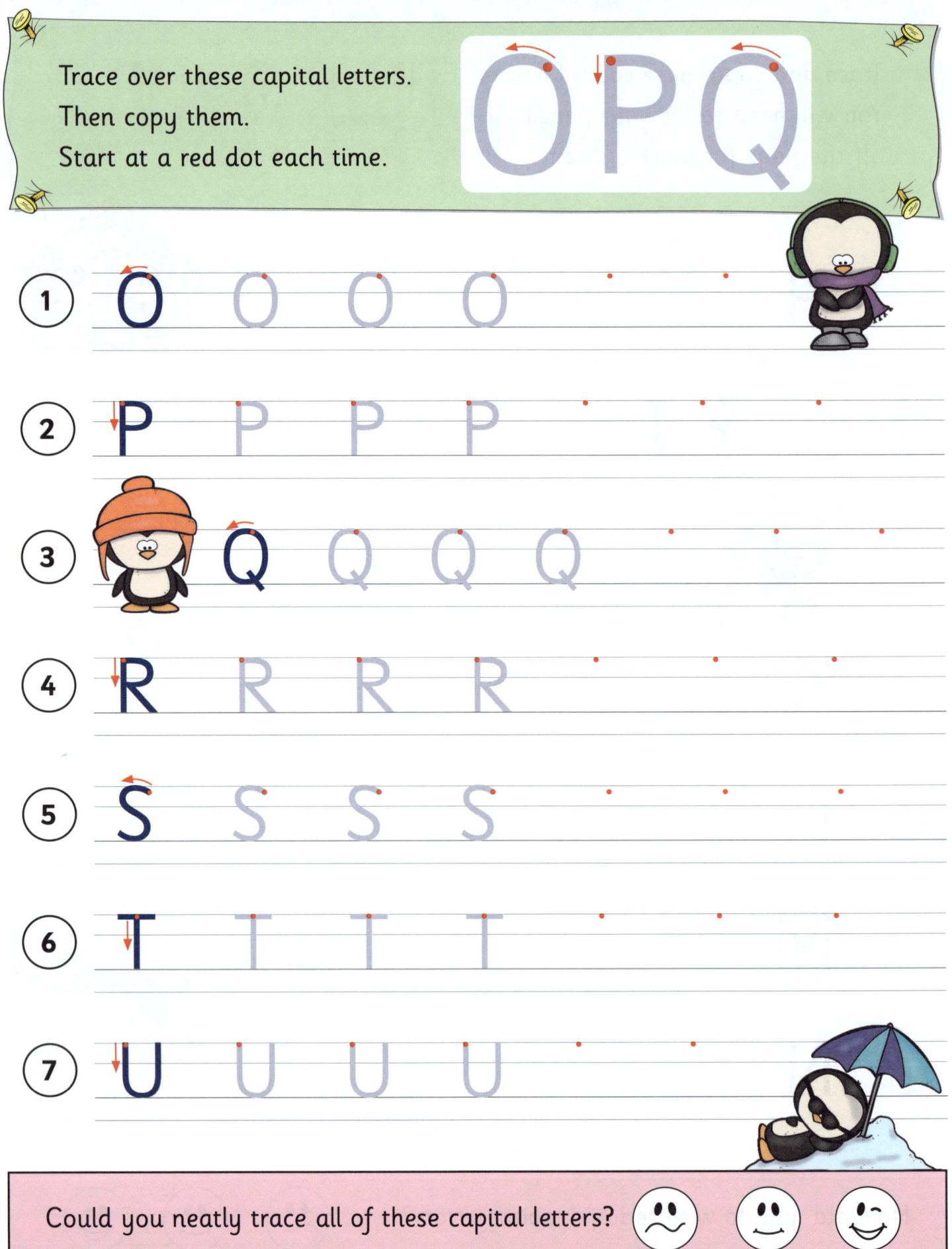

Week 10 — Day 2

Trace and copy the capital letters. Then do the same with the names.

V W

1. V V V V
2. W W W
3. X X X X
4. Y Y Y Y Y
5. Z Z Z Z
6. Ewa   Max
7. Isla   Lucas

How did you get on with this page?

Week 10 — Day 3

Trace and copy these names and places. Make sure your capital letters touch the top line.

1. China   China
2. Ollie   Ollie

3. Italy   Italy
4. Ffion   Ffion
5. Bristol   Bristol
6. Amir   Amir

7. Sydney   Sydney

Were you able to neatly trace these names?

Week 10 — Day 4

Trace and copy the small letters.
Then trace and copy the words below.
All the letters should sit on the thick line.

1. a a
2. i i
3. n n
4. w w 
5. x x
6. zoom   sun 
7. care   oven

Did you copy all of this page correctly?

Week 10 — Day 5

Trace and copy these tall letters. Then try the words with tall letters in them.

1. d d 
2. h h
3. k k 
4. l l 
5. t t
6. tall   head
7. hoof   back

How did you find tracing tall letters?

Week 11 — Day 1

Trace and copy these letters with tails.
Then trace and copy the words.
The letter tails should touch the bottom line.

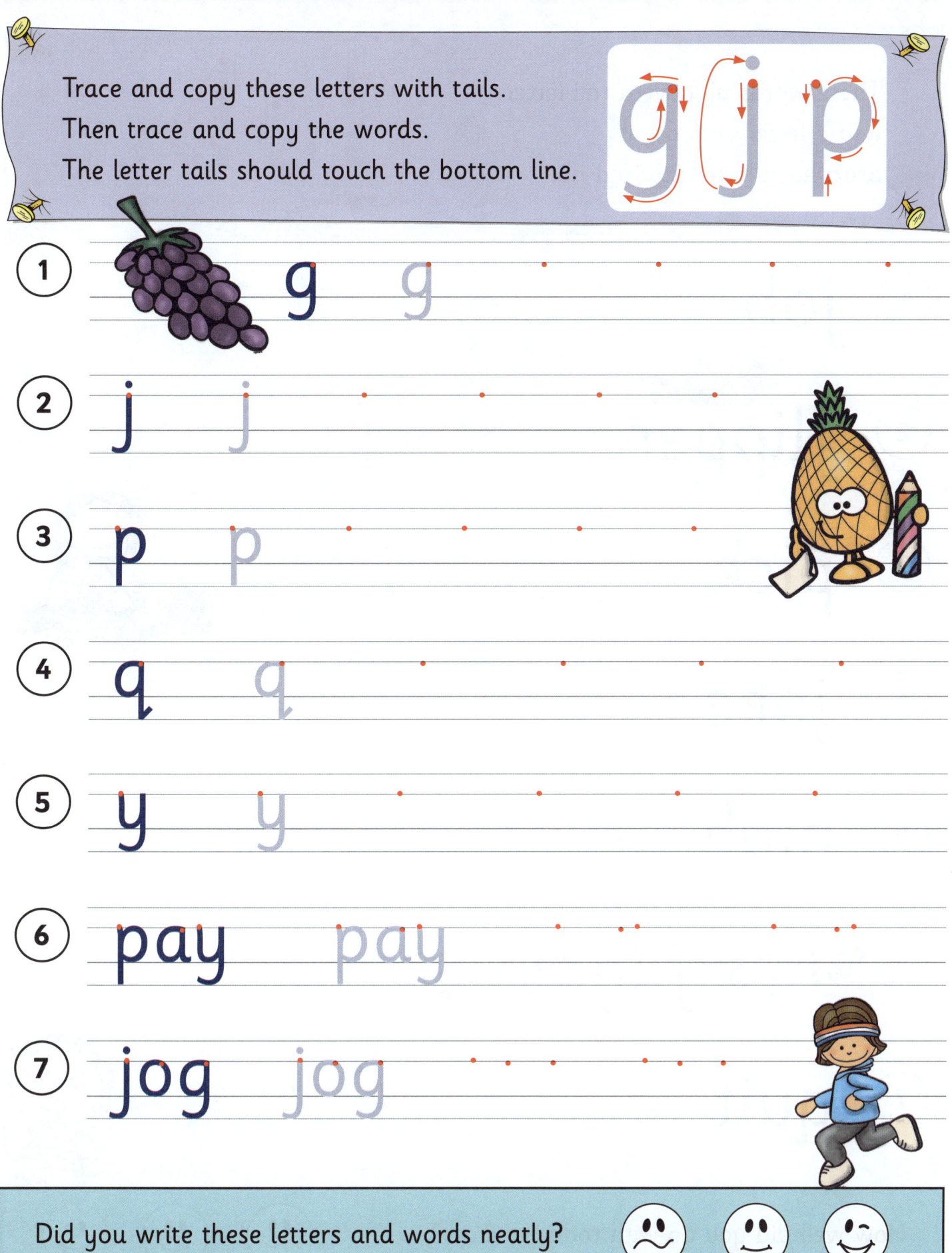

1. g g
2. j j
3. p p
4. q q
5. y y
6. pay pay
7. jog jog

Did you write these letters and words neatly?

Week 11 — Day 2

These words all have a tall letter and a letter with a tail. Start each letter at a red dot.

1. job   job
2. flipper   flipper
3. pick   pick
4. joke   joke
5. high   high
6. flight   flight
7. quit   quit

How well did you do with today's words?

Week 11 — Day 5

Trace and then copy this riddle. Start each letter at a red dot.

A Riddle.

What must you break

before you can use it?

An egg.

Did you copy the riddle neatly?

Week 12 — Day 1

Trace these words first.
Then practise writing them out.

1. the the
2. do do
3. to to

4. here here
5. of of
6. said said
7. says says

How did you find today's words?

Week 12 — Day 2

Trace and then copy the seven words below.
Start each letter at a red dot.

1.  are   are

2. were   were

3. was   was

4. is   is

5. his   his

6. has   has

7. I   I

Were you able to neatly write these words?

Week 12 — Day 3

Here are seven words for you to practise. Trace them first. Then copy them out.

1. you   you
2. your   your
3. he   he
4. she   she
5. be   be
6. me   me
7. we   we

How did you get on with these words?

Week 12 — Day 4

Trace and copy these words.
Make sure to start each letter at a red dot.

1. no   no
2. go   go
3. love   love
4. by   by
5. my   my
6. they   they
7. so   so

How did you find copying these words?

Week 12 — Day 5

Trace this joke. Then copy it out below. Start each letter at a new red dot.

What do you call a cow with a red nose?

Moodolph

How well do you think you did today?

Year 1 Handwriting — Autumn Term